24

MW01242931

...rsion

– The *Non*-OCPD Person
MUST Ask! – *And Have*
Answered!

By **Mack W. Ethridge, NFHR, Inc.**

Award-Winning Writer, Researcher
Educator, Public Speaker

Published by **New Frontier Health Research, Inc.**

Cover design by Mack W. Ethridge

Library of Congress Cataloging-in-Publications, Data, Ethridge, Mack W.

24 Key Questions the *Non*-OCPD Person Must Ask! – Pocket Version
Complete edition

1st Complete Softback Edition, Oct. 2018

Author Qualifications (Partial)

Mack W. Ethridge is a seasoned professional writer/researcher/educator, and life-long psy-chology major, who has devoted thousands of hours to the study of Obsessive-Compulsive Personality Disorder, and draws upon his *first-hand* observations of this disorder in action. He has pioneered methods and techniques of how the <u>Non</u>-OCPD person may best protect themselves from another's OCPD mistreatment, and how the OCPD person may obtain **Insight** into their disorder, paving the road to their recovery, and full enjoyment of Life.

Mack has edited such prestigious periodicals as *The Journal of Neurosurgery*; as well as such notable publications as *The Comprehensive Survey of Doctorate Recipients*, of The National Academy of Sciences; and, as a career editor, has received multiple commendations and awards. Mack has authored 30 OCPD books.

Disclaimer

All instruction or recommendations in this book are not in any fashion to be construed as medical advice, either for physical, psychological, or mental ailments. This research paper is not intended to diagnose the existence of OCPD, nor to prescribe treatment. Nor is it meant to professionally analyze the mental health condition or emotional fitness of the _Non_-OCPD person. Self-assessment tools and related tables for the _Non_-OCPD person (in the source 'Escaping' volume) are provided _only_ to give an overall, general assessment, _likely_ to be reflective of their present capacity to interact with OCPD persons. But, only a qualified mental health practitioner can say for sure. In short, this book is meant for informational purposes, only. Before putting into practice any of its ideas or concepts, you would be well-advised to consult a certified health professional conversant with these matters.

The **Twenty-Four** (24) **KEY Questions** the <u>*Non*</u>-OCPD Person **<u>MUST</u> Ask,** *and* Their **Practical** Answers

Let Us Begin!

What is the *best*, **overall approach** to adopt when dealing and interacting with an OCPD person?

<hr>

No. 1

<hr>

The best overall approach to adopt when dealing with an OCPD person is one of <u>avoiding</u> an argument or conflict or heated disagreement at all costs – *before* it gets a chance to emerge. This is so because such a scenario nearly always leads to much personal distress. Since the OCPD person's nature predisposes them to control, criticize, complain, and attempt to curtail others' rights, these actions of theirs tend to elicit from others annoyed displeasure to angry resistance; to which the OCPD person, in turn, reacts with *even greater* defensive, and then offensive, argumentative and demeaning retaliation. The OCPD person **will** have the last word, they cannot help themselves; which means the argument can only escalate apart from your recognizing this Truth. So, don't fall into their 'trap', rather, be quick to graciously 'bow out' before their ever-present negativity has a chance to 'infect' your being and 'ruin' your day. Better to state your position clearly and confidently, **once**, then *hold* your tongue, rather than to 'bite it' in anger.

What is the *single*, **most important thing** you can do, <u>now</u>, to enhance your relationship with the OCPD person?

_____No. 2_____

The single, most important thing you can do, **now**, to enhance your relationship with the OCPD person is to acquire *as much knowledge as you can* about their unique psychology. This means, primarily, discovering their underlying motivations and their rationale for doing things the way they do. With such vital knowledge, you will be able to 'craft' your response in a way that will prevent the OCPD person from misusing or manipulating you, and allow you to remain free of their tyrannical designs. Knowledge IS power, and never was this more true than in the case of dealing with an OCPD person. Acquisition of *this* specialized knowledge, as revealed in this Research Report, and its consistent and wise application, will work wonders as your proficiency increases.

What is the *principal*, **liberating secret** to remaining calm and composed while on the 'receiving end' of OCPD behavior?

_____No. 3_____

The principal, liberating secret to remaining calm and composed while on the 'receiving end' of OCPD behavior is <u>to</u> <u>have</u> <u>set</u> <u>your</u> <u>intention</u> <u>to</u> <u>do</u> <u>so</u> ***well*** ***before*** coming into contact with the OCPD person. Should you encounter this person, whom you may have come to regard as problematic and an 'interruption' in your life, during the course of your day, you will likely be 'ill-disposed' to greet them and interact with them with any serene 'charity' of spirit, at all. If, however, at the start of your day, before you leave your bedroom, you mentally and orally rehearse as follows: 'I **strongly intend**, _today_, to remain calm and composed in the face of any kind of provocation from the OCPD person,' then, you will stand a much better chance of actually doing it! It is so simple, yet it is **key** to your power!

What is the ***never-failing***, **easily carried out**, **conditioning method** you can utilize to modify an OCPD person's behavior toward you for the good?

The never-failing, easily carried out, conditioning method you can utilize to modify an OCPD person's behavior toward you is that of *the repetition of* the **same** clear, short, and direct, statement, over and over, again, to the *OCPD person's* repeated question or statement. You do not vary its wording, neither do you add or subtract from it. Often, the OCPD person will make the same statement, or ask you the same question, multiple times, at spaced intervals, in an attempt to coerce you to accede to their demands. By your response remaining the identical, consistent, unwavering, the OCPD person will eventually get the message that you are adamant, and that further querying will be to no avail. You, in effect, 'condition', or determine their response. **An example**: Your OCPD spouse tells you she needs more laundry detergent (without saying she _expects_ you to write it down). To which she will _verbally_ mention numerous other items to you throughout the day. You, give the same reply, with every mention of each successive item, as **'Write it on the memorandum'**. Should she protest, say to her, 'You can do it as easily as I can.' Do not deviate from this reply. In time, your spouse will be conditioned to write it down, and not expect you to, relieving her inappropriately of her re-sponsibility to do so. **Another example**: Your relative, or co-worker, brings up a subject of which they are *unnecessarily and overly-concerned*, and desires to discuss it with you, again, perhaps for the 3rd or 4th time. You respond to them by saying, **'We have been through this *before*'**, or **'We have spoken of this *before*'**. Then, remind the OCPD person that the steps necessary to resolve it were also discussed, and **agreed upon**, and that they simply have to implement those steps. Eventually, by your adhering to the same response, the OCPD person will, at some point, recognize this is as far as they are going to get with you, and that it is now up to them, not you, to take responsible action to resolve the matter.

What is the *hidden*, often **un-recognized, motivation** underlying all OCPD behaviors, and how knowing this will empower you?

The hidden, often unrecognized, motivation underlying all OCPD behaviors is the compelling impulse, or desire, for **excellence**. The OCPD person wants more than anything else to give expression to the best that is within them. This is often difficult to perceive due to their unskillful ways of manifesting this worthy and desirable objective. They simply lack the requisite people skills and self-management skills to convey their goal positively and cooperatively and in an attractive manner. Instead of using praise, and humility, and/or an authoritative style that is respectful, they often resort to cold commands, biting criticism, or even a subtle, quietly, but deviously expressed, query intended to usurp your freedom to view things differently, and respond accordingly. Their whole negative approach to others undermines their purpose to achieve excellence, *which isn't excellence!* However, the OCPD person is blind to this. But, if you keep foremost in mind their true, hidden, laudable intention, you will be *much more likely* to respond to them with **understanding**, **admiration**, and a **calm respect**. This does not mean that you will necessarily accede to their demands, but that you will be

empowered to respond with a depth of understanding freeing you from *reactive, un-thinking, 'in-the-dark', non-conciliatory, or a provocative* choice of words and behaviors. In other words, you will be given 'pause', before you reply to the OCPD person, allowing you a 'space' to formulate a kind, gentle, wise, yet a **strong**, self-respecting response, geared to honor the OCPD person, and to honor yourself. Phrases that can prove very helpful in this regard are to say to the OCPD person, 'I **appreciate** your desire to do this in an **excellent** manner, and *I agree with you*,' or 'I recognize you only want to do this in **the best way**, and *I agree with your intention.*' Then, after conveying your appreciative recognition of this fact, the OCPD person will be more open to any observations you have to make on the subject, or modifications you might have to suggest. In short, if the OCPD person feels they are understood (relative to their innermost need, that of excellence), then your interaction with them will oftentimes prove much more fruitful, and harmonious.

What is the *easiest way* **to distract** an OCPD person from their automatic behaviors, freeing you from a distressing situation?

The easiest way to distract an OCPD person from their automatic behaviors is to make use of a psychological tool called *'pattern interrupt'*. Pattern interrupt has to do with breaking the OCPD person's unconscious negative pattern of thought or activity which they are so 'generously sharing' with you! For instance, when the OCPD person begins to complain interminably about the poor treatment by our government of the homeless, or our veterans of foreign wars, you can say to them, 'Oh, *by the way*, did you see the article on our local government *improvement* plan?', or '<u>*Not to change the subject, but*</u> have you heard about how one man has fed two million people worldwide in his lifetime?' The idea, here, is to **re-direct** the OCPD person's attention to another topic, which can be related, but is one that is of a positive nature. Remember, you are not ignoring, nor downplaying the importance of the topics the OCPD person has broached, or their need to be addressed, but due to their unwholesome emphasis upon **only** the negative aspects of those topics, you wisely encourage them to think other thoughts of a more beneficial, edifying nature.

What is the *surprising*, yet **most helpful, reason** you should agree with an OCPD person's *mistaken* beliefs, on occasion?

The surprising, yet helpful, reason you should agree with an OCPD person's mistaken beliefs, on occasion, is, without a shadow of a doubt, to **preserve your peace**. But, by 'agreeing', I do *not* mean *unreservedly* accepting what they say as true. Take for example, the case where an OCPD person very emphatically asserts that 'such and such' is so. It can be anything, but you clearly perceive that the OCPD person has a large emotional investment in his or her position. In such a case, you would be well-advised to respond with, 'You may be right', or 'I think you may have something there,' or 'That is entirely possible'. Statements of this nature are non-combative and non-challenging, and because they are neutral, you stand a much better chance of ensuring a civil interchange with the OCPD person. It allows them to continue talking, if they so choose, without a 'skirmish' occurring between the two of you due to your assertion that their view is highly improbable, if not all wrong. Let them go on believing as they like. You know better.

What is the *one phrase* found to be **most effective** in helping to <u>ensure</u> a harmonious interchange with the OCPD person?

The one phrase found to be most effective in helping to ensure a harmonious interchange with the OCPD person is 'Now, that is <u>very</u> interesting!' This five-word clause accomplishes several things. By reciting this short phrase to the OCPD person regarding any topic they bring up, you *immediately*, and un-mistakably, inform them of your interest in what they have to say. This flatters them, and subsequently, they tend to look more favor-ably upon you, as you *clearly* are smart enough to recognize their intelligence! It relaxes their defenses, and stalls their often-automatic offenses, waiting in the wings to be spring upon you. It doesn't hurt to even repeat this phrase, again, with a little modification, such as, 'How interesting!', or 'Now, you have really got my interest!' Then, after, the OCPD person has pretty much concluded their talk, you can skillfully re-direct the conversation to something more to your liking, and to a subject mutually beneficial.

What is the *optimal* **time of day** to discuss **any sensitive matter** you know the OCPD person will likely emotionally respond to?

_____No. 9_____

The optimal time of day to discuss any sensitive matter you **know** the OCPD person will likely emotionally respond to (in a negative fashion) is that time of day that corresponds to whether they are a *morning*, *afternoon*, or an *evening* person. You would think this would be obvious, but many people disregard this simple, yet profound insight. Every person is so constituted that they function **best** either in the morning hours, afternoon hours, or the evening hours. Their *energy* level, as well as their *patience* levels, not to mention their *cooperative* levels, are at their peak during one of these time periods. It has to do with their own personal **'bio-rhythms'**. To disregard this fact regarding your association with the OCPD person is to do so at your own risk. Through observation, determine which period they function best in, and <u>time</u> your sensitive encounters, if given the opportunity, to coincide with their peak period. By this small action, you are 'stacking the cards' more so in your favor to arrive at a more agreeable interaction.

What *special boundaries* should **you establish** with an OCPD person, you would not <u>ordinarily</u> establish with a normal person?

The special boundaries you should establish with an OCPD person, you would not ordinarily establish (or need to establish) with a normal person, are those boundaries that concern your **personal identity**. This heads the list of all other boundaries because it is the <u>*foundational structure*</u> undergirding the super-structure of all the others. Here is what I mean: If you, the one who associates with the OCPD person do not have a clear, well-defined, and strong understanding and mental picture of *who* you are, in terms of what is important to you, and what you are capable of, you will be **most vulnerable** to the OCPD person **defining you** as they desire you to be, as they see fit. If they believe you to be, or wish you to be, a weak-willed person, confused as to who you are, needing a superior person (the OCPD person, of course!) to enlighten you in your pitiable existence, then, you can be sure the OCPD person will step up to the plate and fulfill that role! You don't want this to happen. So, determine **what** you are about, and hold fast to it! Let no person, least of all the OCPD person, decide **Who** you are. Now, or *ever!*

What *highly beneficial* **length of time** has been demonstrated to be the most favorable relative to quality of an OCPD interaction?

The highly beneficial length of time that has been clearly demonstrated to be the most favorable relative to **quality** of an OCPD interaction is that *prior* length of time after which the OCPD person crosses over from being civil and relatively pleasurable to talk with, to being displeasing and distressing. That period of time can *vary* from OCPD individual to OCPD individual, but for many, it would seem the time frame is, generally speaking, only about fifteen (15) minutes, on average. This is not a fixed and unchanging time period, however. Depending upon a variety of factors impinging upon the OCPD person's mood and disposition, that time period may be significantly longer. It can be much shorter, as well! It is up to you to ascertain what time period would constitute the 'highly beneficial' length of time in your case, meaning what time length can you *safely* and *comfortably* interact with the OCPD person without your becoming upset or disturbed by their speech and actions. As you can imagine, too, your mood also is a big factor in how much time you can spend in the OCPD person's presence without regretting that you did so. Excuse yourself *if* it is in your power to do so.

What *pleasantly*, **unexpected outcome** might your ignoring, or even tolerating, _some_ OCPD traits create for you?

The pleasantly, unexpected outcome of what your ignoring, or even tolerating, some OCPD traits create for you, would be that to your initial surprise, you are likely to realize a greater sense of **self-control** or **self-mastery**. Becoming aware that you do <u>not</u> *always* have to verbally respond to or orally voice your views to the OCPD person can be a liberating experience. You may at first feel the habitual inclination to do so, but once you have refrained from doing so, a heightened sense of freedom can arise in your being. You now see that you do not have to have the last word, defensive or otherwise, and you do not have to enter into a conversation, at all. It is your choice. And you are free to exercise that choice. It can prove to be a welcome delight!

What *overlooked* **methods** **of** 'charm' can be relied upon to help defuse an OCPD confrontation or developing incident?

The overlooked methods of charm that can be relied upon to help defuse an OCPD confrontation or a developing incident are various types of **humor**. But, one has to be careful, here, as every OCPD person, like any other person, has their own _style_ of humor appreciation. With a little experimentation and/or careful observation, though, you will be able to determine what _kind_ of humor the OCPD person is receptive to and enjoys. Just be sure your humor is lighthearted and offered in the sense of goodwill and playful fun. (*Self-depreciation*, or making fun of oneself, can be very effective here, as long as both the OCPD person, and you, realize it is only <u>make</u>-<u>believe</u>!) This, more often than not, serves to lighten the mood of the OCPD person, and open the door to a more comfortable, and profitable interaction. You certainly don't want to engage in humor at the OCPD person's expense, such as any type of juvenile (pranks, name-calling, or childish 'sing-songs') behavior, or sarcasm, where put-downs and unwelcome teasing are utilized. The object is to enhance the relationship through wisdom *<u>and</u>* *<u>wit</u>*, not jokes where a 'just kidding' are supposed to somehow make right.

What *one word* should you **never say** to an OCPD person *under* *any* *circumstance*, even though it's perfectly legitimate and **positive**?

The one word you should never say to the OCPD person under any circumstances is the word, '**preference**'. For if there is one word the OCPD person has tremendous disregard for, it is that word – and all that it stands for! Why is this so? As Sherlock Holmes, that renowned fictional detective, would say, '*Elementary*, my dear Watson!' The OCPD person's lifelong reason for being is to eradicate or 'stamp out' the personal preferences of others! The word 'preference' is a **red flag**, if ever there were one, to be waved before the OCPD person's eyes (*ears* in this case) only at great risk of awakening OCPD traits in their fury! Preference *has reference to* personal choice, personal choice *derives* from autonomy, and autonomy arises from Self-Identity. And it is Self (*unique*) Identity the OCPD person cannot bear, as he wants all others to be *just like himself!* Control by the OCPD person is certainly out of the question, if the non-OCPD person chooses to exercise their preference in all important matters. Save this word for freedom-respecting people.

What *one topic* should you **never discuss** with the OCPD person? (If you think it is politics, or religion, you are *mistaken!*)

_____No. 15_____

The one topic you should never discuss with the OCPD person is the topic (or *topics*) that the OCPD person becomes upset over, angry about, or disturbed by when thinking and conversing. Politics and religion certainly *can* be topics of contention, but they are <u>not</u> necessarily the primary ones. Be observant, listen carefully, and learn what topics are 'off-limits' to broach, and what topics are relatively safe to introduce. For many OCPD persons, topics involving **personal freedom** and **responsibility** can be very tricky, as these are 'hot spots' in the OCPD person's mind. They demand it for themselves, but begrudge others enjoying them. In fact, the OCPD person seeks to deny these to others. Sometimes, the topic can be seemingly the most innocent in the world, but the OCPD person will become riled at its every mention. Only your familiarity with the OCPD person will inform you 'where angels [wisely] fear to tread'. Be like the angels, exercise caution and learn those topics the OCPD person has a fondness for, and limit yourself to those.

What *three main factors* serve to **strengthen** and **enhance** a **romantic relationship** with an OCPD person, and may prove to be *its salvation?*

The three main factors that serve to strengthen and enhance a romantic relationship with an OCPD person from the *non*-OCPD lover's perspective are 1) a ***profoundly*** **deep love** for the OCPD person (and accompanying sorrow over the OCPD person's plight), 2) an ***uncommon*** **commitment** to 'stick it out' and/or a willingness to 'fight for' the continuance and betterment of the relationship, and, 3) an ***extremely*** **high tolerance** for often repeatedly occurring, annoying and disturbing behaviors. Admittedly, these are tall orders. This may come as 'bad news' to some, but better to face the Truth than to pretend such qualities really are not essential. For, without this level, or degree, of love, commitment, and tolerance, the relationship does not stand much of a chance of surviving, much less flourishing. Oh, it may continue on, but in time, any real aspect of romance will wither and die. **This is the hard, cold Truth.** On the bright side, human love **can** grow, become stronger, even under the most distressing circumstances. But, the *non*-OCPD lover must either have, or yet earn, 'high marks' in these areas.

What is the *absolutely* **best way** to contradict or correct the OCPD person when it is absolutely necessary?

_____No. 17_____

The absolutely best way to contradict or correct the OCPD person when it is absolutely necessary is to **preface** your remarks with **conciliatory** gestures. That is, begin your message with words that will tend to placate and appease. In this way, much distrust and animosity on the part of the OCPD person can be overcome. Such goodwill pro-offered at the start will set the tone for your words, citing *their* being mistaken, or outright wrong, to be heard, reflected upon, and seriously considered. And though the OCPD person may exhibit great reluctance to admit their error or fault, only in this way do you stand a chance to 'get through' to the OCPD person. An example of the above might be: 'Terry, I believe your position is fundamentally sound, and workable, but I would strongly *suggest* you think about whether hiring one additional technician would be wise to evaluate its viability.' Or, 'Mary, your plan to carpet only half of the house is laudable in terms of initially saving money, but *don't you think* leaving half of the house without rugs may add substantially to the heating bill?' Approach softly, correct gently!

What Is Your *Greatest* Defense *Against* OCPD Tyranny?

Of all the different strategies and tactics, large and small, offered in this research report to counteract the behaviors of OCPD people, one stands out above all the rest. With this one defense, *alone*, you can safeguard your inner being as though you were securely positioned within a castle of old. No enemy, no invading army, can assault this edifice and breach its walls. It is just too strong and well fortified.

What is this supreme defense? It has been touched upon in this research report, in several sections, but, *now*, needs to be brought to your attention with crystal clarity, utter directness, and a forcefulness that will so impress itself upon your mind that you will never forget it! *Virtually all else within this report could be forgotten*, or rather, you will find yourself doing that 'all else' naturally, even unconsciously, *if* you will but recognize the importance of what I am about to say to you, hold fast to its meaning and power, and live it out in your life each day! That being said, and bearing the foregoing prominently in mind, hear, what to many may be, the surprising answer:

Your greatest defense in dealing with an OCPD person, *or any person*, for that matter, is being perfectly clear about three prime considerations: (1) **Who** you are (who you have *decided* to be), (2) **What** your purpose is (your definite major <u>vocation</u>), and (3) **Why** you exist (why you draw breath each day, your overall reason for being), or what it is you plan to *accomplish* in your brief stay upon earth, as a life goal, in overall terms. This is fundamental. Yet, it seems this vital connection, the overwhelming rel-evance of such answers to how successfully one deals with the OCPD of another, is lost on many of the so-called experts who discuss the perils of OCPD, as they virtually never acknowledge it. It is really all so basic, actually so simple, that most people overlook it entirely. And then they wonder why it is *so hard* to enjoy their day and not be so bothered by others' speech and actions. And, con-sequently, they lose, or never grasp, the one thing that will make of them a veritable 'rock of Gibraltar', or impregnable fortress within! – Where their Peace of Mind can only grow, become stronger, become deeper and more protective, and fulfilling!

If you do _not_ know Who you are, What your purpose is, and Why you exist, then seek to find out. Many excellent resources are available, today, books, DVD's, seminars, etc., that will progressively guide you to discovering your purpose, just waiting for you to avail yourself of them. Make it a priority to discover these great Truths about your being. Nothing could be more important. And, when you do, you will be able to live 'out of your **strength**', rather than out of your *weakness*!

Those other sections within this research report that refer to the above use such terminology as 'a strong sense of identity' (knowing *who* you are), and 'a strong sense of self-worth' (knowing your *value*). And because of their importance, that is **why** you always find such terms *placed at the top* within any narrative discussion or tabular presentation in this research paper.

It is *this* awareness about yourself, your person, your consciousness of your mission (your deliberately reminding yourself of it, your living it out every day), which, **more than anything else**, will set you free from the tyranny of the OCPD's mode of interacting with the world. You will simply be too focused upon your mission to allow outside distractions to upset you. Consequently, the OCPD person will simply have less and *less* impact upon you, creating more sympathy, pity, and compassion for this poor deluded person, as you become more centered in your purpose – and your power – *to be free!*

What should your **primary** objectives be in *any* OCPD relationship interaction?

While in the presence of an OCPD person, and particularly when that person begins to vocally interact with you, and make requests of you, it is of the **utmost importance** that you bear prominently in mind what it is you seek to *specifically* accomplish, what the *desired outcome* is you seek to bring to pass. In other words, what is your **overriding intention** relative to what you hope to **gain** for yourself. Those objectives are numerous, but they are all interrelated. The chief ones are: Preserving your identity, pro-tecting your autonomy (your right to self-determination), establishing and enforcing boundaries, guarding your peace of mind, asserting and defending your God-given rights, maintaining control, taking nothing personally, remaining positive and upbeat, communicating clearly, detecting the OCPD person's underlying motive, recognizing the OCPD person's objective, thinking clearly and accurately, modeling mature, adult behavior, conditioning the OCPD person to conform to your aims, and to become more comfortable in the OCPD person's presence, irrespective of their emotional state.

It is a good idea, at start of day, to mentally rehearse these objectives, _well_ _before_ you come into the presence of the OCPD person. Recite them out loud and repeat them with the strong positive emotions of being **determined** and **resolute** in your desire to achieve these objectives. Refer to your **Primary Objective Reinforcement cards** (found in *'Escaping Another's OCPD Tyranny'*, the source volume for this pocketbook) at strategic times during your day, perhaps just before a business meeting with an OCPD colleague, or shortly before an important discussion with your OCPD relative or mate. Carry the cards with you, or keep them handy in an office desk drawer (better locked!), or in a closet tucked safely away. Note, too, that not all cards necessarily be referred to at once. Select those cards that you feel a need to focus on and firmly implant in your mind, so much so that it becomes 'second nature' to operate from that intention. Picture yourself as achieving these worthy objectives in your mind's eye, carrying out these 'directives'. Then, reap the rewards for your wise diligence!

Is it advisable to seek counsel regarding the *effects* of another's OCPD behavior upon you?

If you are having a <u>very</u> difficult time interacting with an OCPD person, and you do not see any improvement after <u>much</u> time and effort on your part, including your experimenting with various approaches to their disorder; then, it would be highly advantageous for you to consult with a therapist, for yourself.

Further, it is recommended that the therapist (psychologist, psychiatrist, or even a licensed clinical social worker) you choose be **familiar** with OCPD, understanding its unique psycho-logical dynamic, and, preferably, having treated OCPD patients, as well. For even today, many mental health professionals lack knowledge in this area, limiting the value, relevance, and even currency (awareness of latest research) of their advice.

Understand, too, that _many_ people, nowadays, consult mental health professionals, not for any disorder of their own, but, for the knowledge they may gain on another's particular disorder, means to enhance their coping skills, and for better ways to deal with the impositions that the mental illness of another places upon those around them.

And if the solutions they offer prove ineffective, or if for any reason you are not satisfied with a practitioner's competence, manner or style, by all means select another one – as not all mental health professionals subscribe to the same therapeutic approach. The four primary approaches (overall) being psychoanalytic or psycho-dynamic, humanistic/existential, cognitive behavioral, and eclectic.

Know, too, that research has shown that any of the above-cited approaches can be effective when administered by credentialed and well experienced professionals. (Although, cognitive behavioral seems to be the best bet for many.)

And **a final note of caution**: be sure that the therapist is credentialed and licensed in your state. Call your state's health department, your state's psychological association, or consumer affairs to verify same.

What **Distressing** Emotions Are Likely to Arise in You While Experiencing *Another's* OCPD Behavior, and What Are the Ways to Defuse Them?

There are eight emotional groups which consist of the main emotions most people are likely to experience due to another's OCPD behavior. They come in 'couplets', such as *Guilt and Shame*, *Anger and Hate*, *Fear and Intimidation*, *Sadness and Sorrow*, feeling *Trapped and Suffocating*, *Impatience and Loss of Peace*, *Upset and Agitation*, and *Unhappiness and Tears*. The causes, or *triggers*, of these painful emotions vary, but thankfully, the remedies for deliverance from these upsetting feelings, and even their prevention are known, and catalogued for you here. All you have to do is appropriate them (recognize their **freedom-bestowing** and **life-empowering** validity) and avail yourself of the healing 'treatments' provided.

It starts with reading and contemplating scientifically supported and psychologically sound 'meditations', or page-length essays, on a daily basis, on whichever group of emotions that is troubling you. By so doing, you will be *re*-training and *re*-educating your mind to think in new terms (wholly **Truthful** terms) that will allow you to **remove** those unwanted 'states' from your emotional world. Then, subsequent use of the corresponding reminder quick reference pocket cards will reinforce further, at *any* time of need, the states of mind and emotion you need to maintain to be free of emotional distress.

As an example, the emotion of guilt, and its *first-cousin*, shame, are dealt with head on in an easy-to-read, carefully-crafted personal message to you, that will make crystal clear the absolute inapplicability of these most harmful emotions to your person. The attempt of the OCPD person to create these emotions in you, for their own immature, selfish, manipulative, and controlling purposes are wholly uncalled for, unwarranted, and cruel in intention, resulting from a 'little mind' only. You don't have to 'buy into it' ever again! _Nor_ will you! – after studying these liberating concepts herein!

What Situations is It Advisable to Avoid *Altogether* When Dealing with an OCPD Person?

Eating your meals at the same table with the OCPD person   (1 of 7)

Here you risk an unpleasant dining experience, or worse yet, indigestion, because the OCPD person has you there in front of them for a prescribed period of time (the time it takes for you to eat your meal). Sit down at the dinner table <u>only</u> if other people are present, which would be desirable, *if* you choose to share a table with the OCPD person, as there is a greater likelihood that you will not be the sole target for criticism or interrogation. If the OCPD person questions you (which they will) as to why you seldom or never share a meal with them anymore, you may respond with any number of valid reasons, such as:

(1) I am experimenting with different eating schedules, and diets, or, (2) I have discovered that I, often, prefer to eat in solitude, or, (3) I am simply not hungry now, or, (4) I choose not to eat now as I am greatly involved in a personal project, or, (5) tell them directly, but *kindly*, that it seems the topics of conversation that take place at the dinner table are not edifying, or uplifting, to you, and that you prefer not to discuss certain topics while eating. You prefer, instead, a light, relaxed, and upbeat discussion. If that is not possible, it is best that the two

of you eat apart. Perhaps a permanent solution, here, is to re-arrange your eating schedule so that it does not coincide with the OCPD person's eating schedule.

Riding in a vehicle with an OCPD person for any extended period of time

If you have ever been forced to ride with any person with whom you were not on good terms, then you know how uncomfortable and nerve-racking it can be. It is no less difficult when riding with an OCPD person. In fact, it is considerably _more_ difficult!

Here, you are 'trapped' in a small, enclosed compartment, exposed to their every expressed mental aberration, directed at either you or another, but with YOU being the central focus and captive audience! If you are the driver, it actually is **dangerous**, as your alertness is compromised, and you become involuntarily (against your will) preoccupied with the OCPD person's verbally-expressed dysfunctions. They become a great distraction to you while driving, and you are likely to become angry, frustrated, and resentful that you must endure such a distasteful and unpleasant situation. It is better to keep such shared rides to a bare minimum, of the *shortest* duration possible, and to have ready reasons (prepared beforehand) why you cannot take the OCPD person somewhere, or go with them. The one exception to the above is that *if* there are other passengers, you may choose to go along, as this may ameliorate, or encourage better behavior from the OCPD person.

Sitting down in a living room (den or recreation room) with an OCPD person for any extended period of time (3 of 7)

It seems that the longer you are in the presence of an OCPD person, the greater is the likelihood that their OCPD behaviors will emerge full-blown. For example, even attempting to relax on a couch with an OCPD person next to you in a recliner, who is reading the newspaper, can prove to

be a very disagreeable experience. Often this person will begin to read out loud all of the terrible things that are going on in the world! They will rehearse all of the tragedies taking place between movie stars! They will recite all of the government blunders and con-gressional members' character failings and illegalities! – All the while expressing disgust upon their face and horror or shock or anger in their tone of voice! Just the thing you need at the end of a hectic or demanding or stressful day! So avoid this! Keep your contact in this setting to a minimum. And at the first sign of aberrant behavior and speech, excuse yourself from the room on any pretext that is logical and convincing.

If you have not already experienced such a 'getaway', you are likely to be in for a great, though unwelcome, surprise! OCPD people do not infrequently use such a trip as an opportunity to 'showcase' all of their OCPD dysfunctional behaviors. Examples include: Planning every street to go down, in the precise sequence of their choosing; scheduling every restaurant (only they possess the culinary experience to determine the best) and museums to visit (only they have the historical or cultural expertise to select the most educational); or touring which beach houses or motels are the most economical and/or esthetically appealing places for lodging. And, of course, your being 'confined' in such close quarters with an OCPD person in both the vehicle while traveling *and* the residence (if the same room, or same apartment) will likely prove to be more than you bargained for in terms of feeling at ease, being comfortable, and being able to relax in their company. If you expected to be able to relax and 'unwind', don't. Such an adventure could well be disastrous to the unknowledgeable, unskilled, or un-initiated!

Waiting in a foyer, lobby, or waiting room with an OCPD person for any extended period of time (5 of 7)

Here, again, you are setting yourself up for a barrage of unwelcome dialogue which neither interests you, nor is edifying for you. OCPD people can be quite talkative, and you being the only one there with them are certain to get an earful of whatever they wish to put a negative slant on! If you find you are thrust into such a situation, be prepared with reasons to excuse yourself, such as you will just 'browse around the area' for a while, or you need to 'stretch your legs' and get some exercise. Also, it is a good idea to have some reading materials upon your person – a small 'pocket-sized book', a handy cross-word puzzle, or even an MP3 player with headphones in your pocket.

You are highly advised *not* to answer your cell phone when you recognize by caller ID that the person trying to reach you is an OCPD person. Resist the temptation to answer the ring, and simply let the caller leave a message, which they will do if it carries any importance. Then, at a time of your convenience, access the call and listen to what the OCPD person has to say. You can then decide, in uninterrupted quietude, how to best respond. You might even wisely choose to phone the OCPD person back when you know they will be unavailable to answer, allowing you to leave a reply message without having to speak to the person directly. Is this going to extremes? Does this sound like an unnecessary practice, even a nonsensical one? – The answer is an emphatic – **_No_**! Why is this? Well, the wholly rational and peace-protecting reasoning behind it is as follows: Should you answer the call, you will at once be a 'captive audience' (at least for the duration of the call) as you are subjected to a conversation that may or *may not* be satisfying, beneficial, or productive. (Reflection on your past history of calls with the OCPD person will disclose the likelihood of this.) Here, you open yourself up to having directives 'fired at you', being 'cross-examined' as to your current activities, and being the recipient of a negative stream of argumentative dialogue that can only serve to devalue the quality of your day. Therefore, I strongly suggest you implement this practice, and reap the benefits of *your* being in control of the interaction, which could easily become unwelcome and distressing, otherwise.

Staying in your home office to read extensively, write, do research, place phone calls, etc., related to your work-at-home employment when the OCPD person is in the house, or in the apartment (7 of 7)

Again, as in the foregoing sections 'Sitting down in your living room (den or recreation room)' or 'Waiting in a foyer, lobby', etc., you are placing yourself in a situation where access to you is immediate and out of your control. Your OCPD housemate or spouse may view your working arrangement as one where they would have frequent and open access to you whenever they please, which due to the OCPD person's dysfunctional proclivities, would probably not be wise to allow. (Try it, you'll see!) *If*, however, you can make it abundantly clear that while you are in your home office, you are <u>not</u> to be disturbed for **any** reasons other than *safety, health*, or *security reasons* or *concerns*, or emergencies, and the OCPD person will <u>fully</u> cooperate, then by all means, take advantage of your convenient home-work setting.

But, should you find that the OCPD person is unable to keep their promise to respect your wishes in this matter, and he or she makes frequent intrusions into your work space (bearing their distressing views and distorted perceptions, of course!), then you have the option of taking your laptop and books to a local library, a college study hall, a vacant university lecture room, a church reading room, a shopping mall, a motel or hotel lobby, a quiet cafeteria or restaurant, a museum or art gallery, or even to a friend or relative's house where you can work uninterrupted and in peace. Even working in your vehicle is an option preferable to what

OCPD stress you would encounter at home! And don't forget that you can go to a local outdoor park or garden during pleasant weather, and complete your work on a park bench, lawn chair, or blanket. The choice is yours.

Are OCPD People Ever a **Danger** to Themselves, *or to Others*?

As had already been stated at the start of this Research Report, OCPD behaviors *can be* nothing short of disastrous. Cited were physical spousal abuse, nervous breakdowns, marital discord, estrangement, divorce, children deprived of one of their parents, and even suicide. Yet, **other very real dangers exist** for the individual who is bombarded by the OCPD's unrestrained actions. What might they be? Well, a person can become *so* upset, *so* agitated, *so* nervous, about the prospect of having to continually deal with an OCPD person, that the resulting distraction and preoccupation about the matter *compromises* their ability to drive safely, to operate machines cautiously, or to make sound judgments (to think clearly) relative to the daily affairs of life. Just how many car accidents, machine injuries, and other unfortunate happenings occur, will never be known, but you can be sure the number is high – *All* resulting from the mental illness 'influences' of another's OCPD 'overtaking' and adversely impacting the life of its undeserving 'victim'. Of course, in addition to the danger of physical harm, or loss of life, the 'victim' runs the risk of developing mental disorders of their own (formerly called 'complexes'), if they have any predisposition to do so, due to the tremendous, inordinate, and un-relieved stress they can be under. This is not a desirable prospect to contemplate, but it is nonetheless a distinct possibility for some. As you can see, OCPD can have **serious consequences** for all parties involved, unless the matter is dealt with decisively, courageously, and most important, knowledgeably. To deny this possibility, though remote, is to do so at your own risk.

It is *far better* to acknowledge the possibility, and then to take those necessary steps of gaining specialized knowledge and expertise in dealing with another's OCPD disorder, than to allow such a possibility to become a reality, from which only regret and heartache can result.

What Physical Health Problems Is One More Susceptible to Due to a Close and Ongoing Relationship with an OCPD Person?

As if all of the mental, emotional, and psychological stress and strain were not enough in your interactions with the OCPD person, you must also be aware of the **very real** physical health dangers. Not only is the *non*-OCPD person at greater risk for headaches (including migraines), neck aches, backaches, severe stomach aches, duodenal ulcers, acid reflux disease, abdominal difficulties, such as possibly even the aggravation of irritable bowel syndrome, but also higher blood pressure, and even a greater risk for cardiovascular problems, including heart attacks. For example, it has only fairly recently been scientifically proven that the emotion of grief can have extremely detrimental effects on the organ of the heart, and can actually precipitate myocardial infarction, or a heart attack. This has been referred to as 'The Broken Heart Syndrome', wherein, apparently, the immune system of the grieving party is also compromised and contributes to the deterioration of health of the *non*-OCPD person. And, as has been shown in this Research Report, grief, or bereavement, is not infrequently a very powerful emotion that a *non*-OCPD person feels toward 'losing' what could have been a normally nurturing and health-fortifying relationship with, for example, a sibling, or even romantic partner. Some *non*-OCPD persons even describe their feelings precisely as those emotions they would experience for the <u>demise</u> of a dearly departed loved one. While it is true the two people still interact, it feels *as though* the OCPD person has truly died, and those feelings of grief are just as strong as if the OCPD person *actually* did die! This being the case, there is every logical reason to believe the cardio-vascular system of the greatly distressed *non*-OCPD person is at a much higher risk for damage, as well, even though no empirical (concrete) evidence is available to prove this distinct possibility, as yet.

What You Can Be Sure *Will Happen* If You Do **Not** Learn *All You Can* About the OCPD Person's Disorder?

_____No. 25_____

When confronting **any** mental disorder, to be *without* sound and accurate knowledge of its nature, its typical course of development, and its ultimate prognosis, or outcome, is to be at its mercy. For it is only through understanding any given mental disorder's underlying causes and predictable manifestations that a person can *begin* to know how to best interact with such a person, and to prevent or alleviate any distressing emotions sure to otherwise arise. This is certainly every bit the case with OCPD.

ODPD, if not treated, tends to worsen over time. It will not get better on its own. Nor should you expect it to – given the fact that the negative traits OCPD people routinely exhibit seem to arise from a kind of 'hard-wiring' within their brain to think and act the way they do. It is 'natural' and 'normal' for them to do so. That is why they are so hard to 'reach' relative to affording them insight into their dysfunctional behaviors, either by their loved ones, or medical professionals, themselves. For them to be told THEY are the problem, and not others, is to **invert** their whole understanding of reality, *as they see it*, and, for some, this is the equivalent of entering 'The Twilight Zone'! – A catch phrase originating back in the 60's that referred to a person crossing over into a realm where the known laws of the universe no longer applied.

Given the above, you can readily see that your situation with the OCPD person does not stand a *chance* of improvement without your acquiring **specialized knowledge** gained at great expense and effort from a select group of scientists, researchers, and lay people who have studied this phenomena extensively, and compelled nature to yield up her secrets of how to 'normalize' relations with OCPD people to the greatest extent possible. It is available, now, to take advantage of. You need only do it.

What Should I Tell Others About my Loved One's, Friend's, or Co-Worker's OCPD Condition?

_____No. 26_____

There may be times when it will be necessary for you to tell others of this person's disorder. Perhaps, your close friends are confused or perplexed about your loved one's behavior. Maybe your co-workers are feeling the strain of daily intercourse with this person, and the team effort there is being compromised. Or, perhaps a medical professional with whom the OCPD person must interest needs to be informed of their mental condition to properly understand, evaluate, and treat them. You, being their concerned relative or associate, would have a desire (if not an obligation) to relate this information to the health provider, or at least to satisfy yourself that they are *aware* of it. (The OCPD person is, often, unlikely to volunteer this information.)

There is no need, however, to feel ashamed, or embarrassed, or even guilty, that your loved one or friend or associate is mentally ill. As the stigma which was once associated with this term is, now, to many, nonexistent, due to the 'demystification' of mental illness, and the dismantlement of superstitions associated with it, through modern science, research, and rational thought.

If you choose <u>not</u> to use the term 'mentally ill', then by all means, you are not obligated to do so. Say, instead, that they have a **'mental health issue'** or **'a chemical imbalance in the brain'**, or they have a **personality disorder**, or an **emotional disorder**, or even a **thinking disorder**. You may simply leave it at saying a **'medical condition** which affects their perception and behavior,' if you choose. Any of these phrases would be accurate, but use whichever one you feel most comfortable with. Then respond to any questions for clarification as you feel appropriate.

The intent, here, is simply to responsibly inform another, for *their* benefit, that this person has a problem that interferes with normal functioning and the quality of interpersonal relationships. If the OCPD person possessed 'insight', they would surely thank you for it.

Is It *Really* Necessary to Categorize (Pigeon Hole) this Controlling, Perfectionistic, Rights-Disregarding, and otherwise Mentally-Ill Person?

_____No. 27_____

At this point, it might be helpful to some of our readers to comment on the 'labeling' of this mentally ill person, or of placing such people in categories, as the intent is <u>not</u> to stigmatize, depreciate, or lessen their intrinsic worth as human beings, but rather to utilize a semantic tool which will prove helpful in the long run of empowering those who interact with the OCPD person to call forth from within themselves a more caring and mature response.

As Dr. Robert M. Bramson, Ph.D., author of *Coping with Difficult People*, a Ballantine publication (pages 138-139), has this to say, 'Most people feel an inner resistance to the idea of categorizing people, putting them in boxes labeled 'Difficult People,' 'Indecisive,' 'Complainer,' or whatever. . . But. . . there [are] some very practical reasons for categorizing people.'

The first reason 'is that labeling people often helps you feel 'distanced' from them, especially if they're people with whom you're very involved. It allows you to see their behavior as happening outside of yourself and your personal responses. That is, it often enables you to see that the Hostile-Aggressive person or the Complainer isn't being hostile or complaining just with you, but that he or she does this to everyone in similar situations. Identifying the *kind* of Difficult Person you've encountered can in itself help you to take the disturbing behavior less personally. You become less paralyzed wondering what you did to bring it on and become more ready for an active, more efficient response.'

The second reason is that by categorizing people 'you may gain an insight into their behavior. . . Thus, just recognizing that they are habitually indecisive [for example] tells you something about them.'

'It is important, however, that you see the labels and the behavior patterns they describe as *prototypes* [dealing with unique individuals], rather than *stereotypes* [dealing with non-descript persons who are uniformly, without variation, the same].'

So let nothing within this research report be taken to mean *anything other* than respect and compassion for the OCPD person, as this is their due by birthright as a fellow human being.

And that having been said, remember the respect and compassion *due unto yourself*, as you become increasingly more proficient in successfully dealing with the OCPD person's dysfunctional speech patterns, actions, and reactions.

What is the <u>Central</u>, Major **Ethical Dilemma** for Many Dealing with OCPD People – and Its *Resolution?*

_____No. 28_____

A very real problem exists in the minds of many ethical people who are burdened with the thought of obligation to OCPD people, especially their close family members. They sincerely believe that no matter *how* disrespectful their OCPD family member is of them, they still are obligated to endure it. No matter *how* controlling and critical of them their OCPD relative is, they must bear up under it, silently and without offering resistance. No matter *how* demanding and manipulative their kin are to them, they feel 'honor-bound' to bear the brunt of their OCPD mistreatment. It seems that *nothing* could be said, nor *any* act committed, that would *disqualify* the OCPD person from receiving allegiance from their concerned, caring, and devoted loved one. Nothing the OCPD person could do that would forfeit another's loyalty to their person, irrespective of the damage and harm the OCPD person was inflicting upon them. Is this thinking accurate, or is it flawed in some manner – relative to sound morality and virtuous conduct? Let us see.

What must be clearly understood is that a loved one has a responsibility _**to**_ their family member, but they do _**not**_ have a responsibility *__for__* that family member. This means that every individual is responsible *for themselves*, OCPD people being no exception. For their thoughts, their feelings, their actions. Even those thoughts, feelings, and actions that are maladaptive and dysfunctional and seemingly automatic, or un-controllable! This is crucial to grasp if you are to be free from the erroneous idea that their welfare, their sense of well-being, is *more important* than your own. It is NOT more important! *Equally* important, YES! More important, NO! This assessment is mature, balanced in its concern and consideration for all involved, unselfish, and fair. It is in accord with sanity and reason, and the dictates of life regarding the law of self-preservation. Once you fully see the 'charitableness' of this view, the liberalness of giving to all people of 'need', *including yourself*, then you can make appropriate decisions that will no longer 'enable' or 'encourage' your relative's dysfunctional behavior. For you are **not** responsible for their behavior. You did not create it. You do not compel them to act as they do. They are responsible for their behavior, *solely*.

Now, that being said, you can continue to do *all you can do* to comply with all *reasonable* requests of your OCPD relative, should you choose, but firmly refuse to agree to any unreasonable ones. Once you have adopted this stance, and demonstrated that your change in response toward them is permanent, your OCPD relative will see you mean business, and eventually (usually fairly soon), he or she will alter their behavior, in a favorable manner, to the new conditions facing them. And, then, the quality of your relationship with them will never be the same – as before!

Dr. Robert M. Bramson, Ph.D, in his book *Coping With Difficult People. . . In Business and in Life*, page 147, reminds us to 'Remember, **no one** is under a moral obligation to remain in the vicinity of, to keep working with, **or even to keep living with**, another person whose behavior is demoralizing, severely upsetting, or stress-producing. I emphasize this point because *I keep finding people for whom it is not obvious at all*. They confuse a practical question of costs and benefits with a moral imperative.' [emphasis mine, throughout]

Dr. Bramson is right. Don't you be one of those people! Do whatever you need to do to ensure and protect your sense of well-being, peace of mind, and sanity! If this means ultimately living apart from your loved one or relative, then by all means do so! Do not live your life under the false belief that your *blood-tie* to another person morally obligates you to a close and unbreakable connection with that person, even though that person may have 'special needs.' To continue to do so is to live a life of 'co-dependency', which is where each other's habitual actions serve to perpetuate an unhealthful, and abnormal, interaction between two people. So, friend, hear this loud and clear: It is right, appropriate, and moral for *your* legitimate needs to be addressed and met. By doing so, you'll be in a <u>*much*</u> better emotional and psychological position to assist your loved one with your now *more readily accessible* inner resources and love!

Farewell Message

Dear friend,

Congratulations! You have now completed your survey of twenty-four of the most **basic**, yet _critical_, questions concerning OCPD, and their highly practical answers. This fundamental education will stand you in good stead as you incorporate these solutions into your daily life. It is my sincere hope that you will, now, if not already having done so, obtain my flagship volume, **Escaping Another's OCPD Tyranny**, from which these vital questions and answers were derived. And having done the above, you have journeyed _far_ in your undertaking to complete the full course of instruction and make it an active part of your life. You will rightfully be very proud that you have done so. You will have looked deep into wellsprings of knowledge, courageously examining the validity or falsity of *long-held* assumptions, opinions, beliefs, and attitudes, about yourself, and the OCPD person, as difficult as that was, or will be, at times, and searched your soul to arrive at the Truth of the 'whys' and 'wherefores' of the OCPD individual's life, as well as your own. And though you will feel, perhaps, uncomfortable on occasion in doing so, you will have 'stayed the course' and confronted the OCPD sufferer's deepest insecurities, false pride, arrogance, adult regressive tendencies (childishness), inaccurate thinking, and even outright ignorance in some cases, again, on the OCPD person's part. But, no matter, for as that early 20th century American sage, Will Rogers, once said, 'We are **all** ignorant, but not about the same things.' However, as regards the Obsessive Compulsive Personality Disorder, that will no longer be said of you to your great credit. For after your having read this book, and *'Escaping'*, its source volume, studiously, and with an open mind, you will now know far more about this subject than *ninety-nine* percent of all other people. And, more importantly, you will possess the intellectual and psychological tools required to ***successfully* confront** this formidable disorder *head-on* whenever it should seek to control and enslave you by the speech, actions, and/or behavior of the OCPD afflicted person.

The source volume of 'Escaping' begins in its Introduction with a hearty 'Congratulations' to you for having wisely chosen to purchase it as 'one of the best investments of your life'. Let this pocket book, now, come to a close with an equally-sincere, even more hearty: '**Congratulations!**' You will have, without a doubt, earned it as you make steady progress toward **freeing yourself** from the disrespect, harass-ment, and tyranny of such an OCPD individual who suffers almost as much as those accosted by them.

And, from this point on, refer back to this book periodically as an advocate for **clear**, **accurate**, **mature**, wholly **sane thinking**. Thinking that upholds the principles of _your_ personal liberty, autonomy, self-determination, and the freedom to decide your own way, even in the seemingly 'little things' of everyday household and workplace life. For by being fully conscious of these 'inalienable rights' which belong to all individuals, you, my now-wiser friend, will ensure those same rights – for yourself. Godspeed!

Mack W. Ethridge
President, NFHR, Inc.

Remember!

YOU Are **Deserving** of **Respect** and **Honor** as a Human Being Made in the **Image** of the **Divine! Never** Permit **a Mentally Ill OCPD Person to** Usurp Your *God-Given* **Freedoms! Defend** Yourself, with Dignity, – and **Stay Free!**

Parting Thoughts

We, here, at
**New Frontier Health
Research, Inc.,**

Thank you _sincerely_ for
the opportunity to serve!

We strive to be _ever-the-more_ deserving of your
trust and **patronage**
through our ongoing study
and research.

24 <u>KEY</u> QUESTIONS

The *Non*-OCPD Person <u>MUST</u> Ask!

(And *Have* Answered!)

Finis

Excerpted from

Escaping Another's OCPD Tyranny! (Textbook Volume)

Comments welcome!

mackethridge@hotmail.com

Made in the USA
Middletown, DE
20 August 2022